ALL Jazzed Up!
INTERMEDIATE PIANO SOLO

MOTOWN

T0065911

ISBN 978-1-4950-6993-2

7777 W. BLUEMOUND RD. P.O. BOX 13819 MILWAUKEE, WI 53213

In Australia Contact:
Hal Leonard Australia Pty. Ltd.
4 Lentara Court
Cheltenham, Victoria, 3192 Australia
Email: ausadmin@halleonard.com.au

Visit Hal Leonard Online at
www.halleonard.com

HOW SWEET IT IS
(To Be Loved by You)

Words and Music by EDWARD HOLLAND,
LAMONT DOZIER and BRIAN HOLLAND

rit.

AIN'T NOTHING LIKE THE REAL THING

Words and Music by NICKOLAS ASHFORD
and VALERIE SIMPSON

Moderately fast

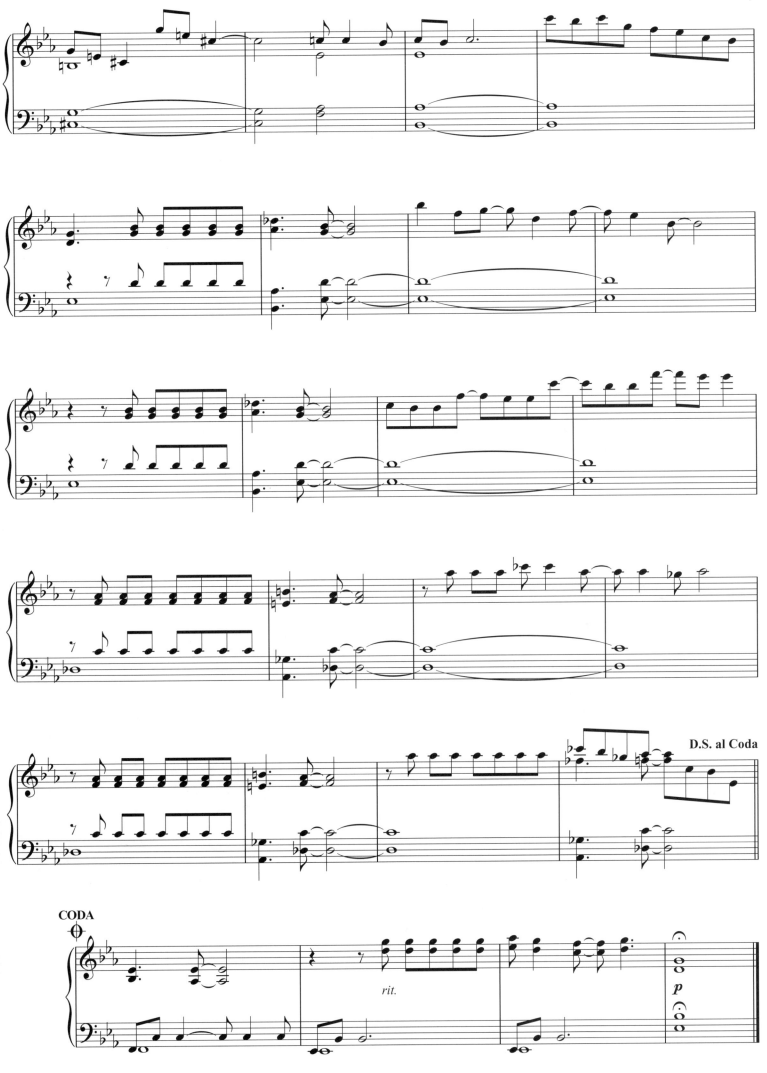

I CAN'T HELP MYSELF

(Sugar Pie, Honey Bunch)

Words and Music by BRIAN HOLLAND,
LAMONT DOZIER and EDWARD HOLLAND JR.

D.S. al Coda

CODA

I HEARD IT THROUGH THE GRAPEVINE

Words and Music by NORMAN J. WHITFIELD
and BARRETT STRONG

MY GIRL

Words and Music by SMOKEY ROBINSON
and RONALD WHITE

I WANT YOU BACK

Words and Music by FREDDIE PERREN, ALPHONSO MIZELL,
BERRY GORDY JR. and DEKE RICHARDS

LET'S GET IT ON

Words and Music by MARVIN GAYE
and ED TOWNSEND

D.S. al Coda

CODA

NEVER CAN SAY GOODBYE

Words and Music by
CLIFTON DAVIS

To Coda ⊕

D.C. al Coda
(take 2nd ending)

CODA

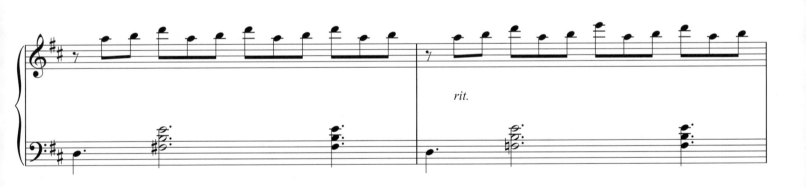

rit.

OVERJOYED

Words and Music by
STEVIE WONDER

STILL

Words and Music by
LIONEL RICHIE

Moderately slow Ballad

YOU CAN'T HURRY LOVE

Words and Music by EDWARD HOLLAND JR.,
LAMONT DOZIER and BRIAN HOLLAND

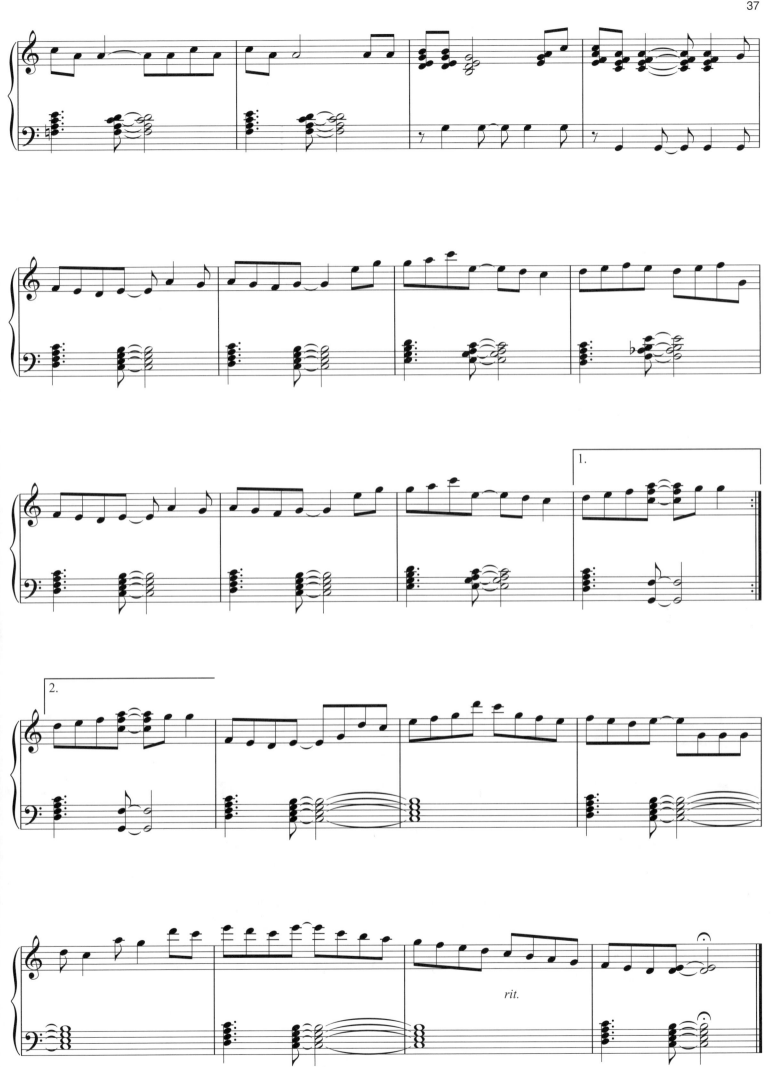

PAPA WAS A ROLLIN' STONE

Words and Music by NORMAN WHITFIELD
and BARRETT STRONG